School Days

Fabiola Sepulveda

2.10

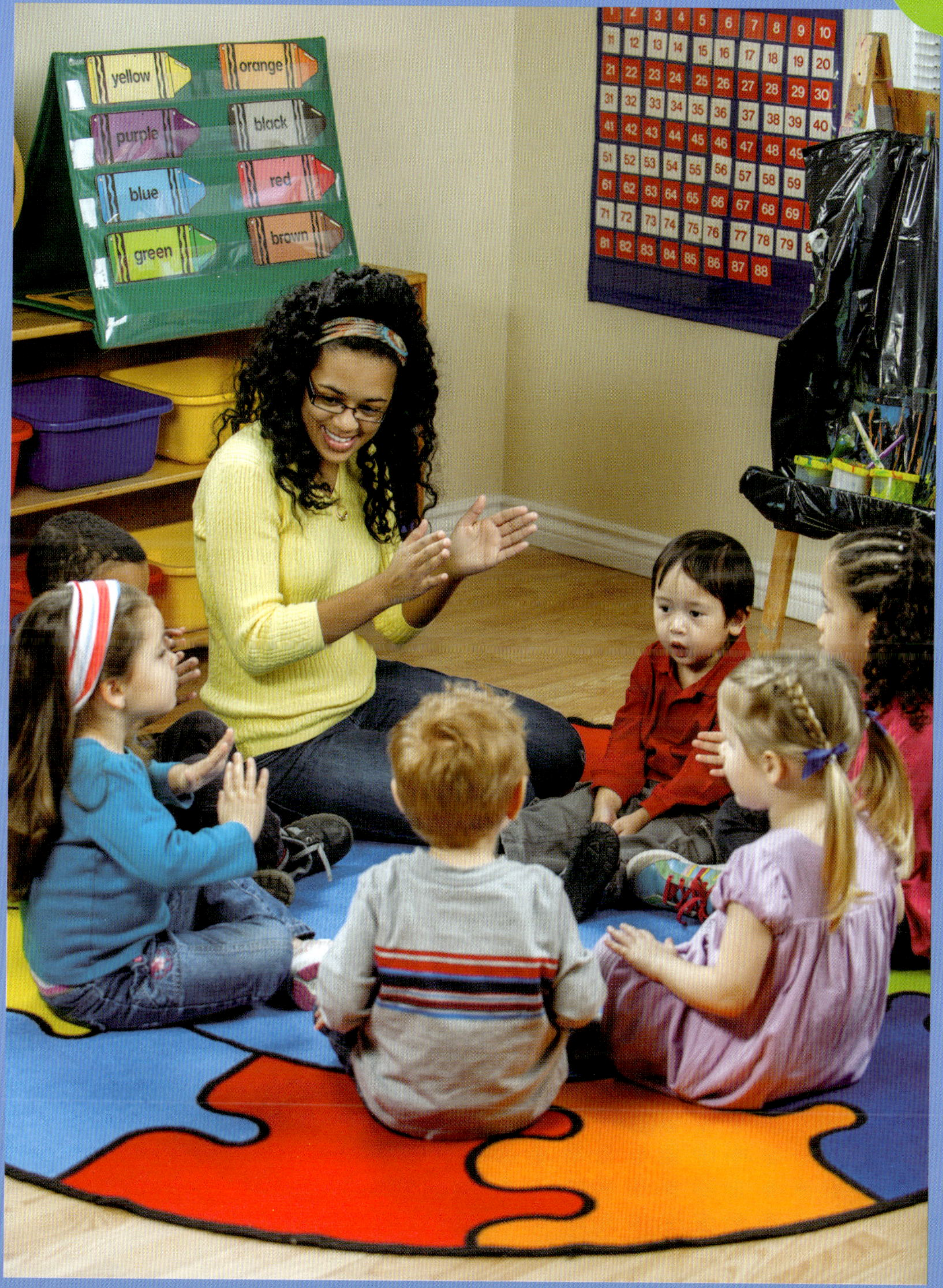
yellow
orange
purple
black
blue
red
green
brown

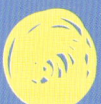

Notes for the Grown-ups

This wordless book allows for a rich shared reading experience for children who do not yet know how to read words or who are beginning to learn. Children can look at the pages to gather information from what they see, and they can suggest text to tell the story.

To extend this reading experience, do one or more of the following:

Find or draw more pictures to show what happens during school days.

Introduce vocabulary such as these words when looking at the pictures and telling the story you see:

- art
- learn
- lunch
- math
- play
- reading
- recess
- school
- sharing
- students
- teacher
- time

Ask the child all the things they do at school each day and which are their favorite things.

After reading the pictures, come back to the book again and again. Rereading is an excellent tool for building literacy skills.

Tell each other the story of one of your favorite school memories.

Consultant

Cynthia Malo, M.A.Ed.

Publishing Credits

Rachelle Cracchiolo, M.S.Ed., *Publisher*
Emily R. Smith, M.A.Ed., *SVP of Content Development*
Véronique Bos, *VP of Creative*
Dona Herweck Rice, *Senior Content Manager*

Image Credits: all images from iStock and/or Shutterstock

Library of Congress Cataloging in Publication Control Number:
2024007560

5482 Argosy Avenue
Huntington Beach, CA 92649
www.tcmpub.com
ISBN 979-8-7659-6130-8
© 2025 Teacher Created Materials, Inc.
Printed by: 926. Printed in: Malaysia. PO#: PO11723